Technology through the Ages

TRANSPORTATION
THROUGH THE AGES

From Stirrups to Steam

MICHAEL WOODS AND MARY B. WOODS

TWENTY-FIRST CENTURY BOOKS / MINNEAPOLIS

For Alexander Woods

Twenty-First Century Books™
An imprint of Lerner Publishing Group, Inc.
241 First Avenue North
Minneapolis, MN 55401 USA

For reading levels and more information, look up this title at www.lernerbooks.com.

Main body text set in Bembo Std Regular.
Typeface provided by Monotype Typography.

Library of Congress Cataloging-in-Publication Data

Names: Woods, Michael, 1946–author. | Woods, Mary B. (Mary Boyle), 1946–author.
Title: Transportation through the ages : from stirrups to steam / Michael Woods and Mary B. Woods.
Description: Minneapolis : Twenty-First Century Books, [2025] | Series: Technology through the ages | Includes bibliographical references and index. | Audience: Ages 11–18 | Audience: Grades 7–9 | Summary: "Since the first humans began to spread around the world, people have been developing new ways to move themselves and their possessions. From wheels to warships, follow the development of transportation technology throughout the ancient world"—Provided by publisher.
Identifiers: LCCN 2023048872 (print) | LCCN 2023048873 (ebook) | ISBN 9798765610091 (library binding) | ISBN 9798765629925 (paperback) | ISBN 9798765638972 (epub)
Subjects: LCSH: Transportation engineering—History—To 1500—Juvenile literature.
Classification: LCC TA1149 .W667 2025 (print) | LCC TA1149 (ebook) | DDC 629.0409—dc23/eng/20231213

LC record available at https://lccn.loc.gov/2023048872
LC ebook record available at https://lccn.loc.gov/2023048873

Manufactured in the United States of America
1 – CG – 7/15/24

CONTENTS

INTRODUCTION ---------------------------------- 4

CHAPTER ONE
TRANSPORTATION BASICS ------------- 7

CHAPTER TWO
THE ANCIENT MIDDLE EAST ----------- 16

CHAPTER THREE
ANCIENT EGYPT ------------------------- 24

CHAPTER FOUR
ANCIENT CHINA ------------------------- 32

CHAPTER FIVE
ANCIENT INDIA -------------------------- 38

CHAPTER SIX
THE ANCIENT AMERICAS ------------- 44

CHAPTER SEVEN
ANCIENT GREECE ----------------------- 52

CHAPTER EIGHT
ANCIENT ROME ------------------------- 58

CONCLUSION
AFTER THE ANCIENTS --------------- 63

Timeline ------------------------------------ 70
Glossary ------------------------------------ 72
Source Notes------------------------------- 74
Selected Bibliography--------------------- 75
Further Reading --------------------------- 76
Index --------------------------------------- 78

INTRODUCTION

What do you think of when you hear the word *technology*? You probably think of something totally new. You might think of research laboratories filled with computers, microscopes, and other scientific tools. But technology doesn't just refer to brand-new machines and discoveries. Technology is as old as human society.

Technology is the use of knowledge, inventions, and discoveries to make life better. The word *technology* comes from Greek. *Tekhne* means "art" or "craft." Adding the suffix *-logia* meant "the study of arts and crafts." In modern times, the word usually refers to a craft, technique, or tool itself. There are many forms of technology. Medicine is one form. Agriculture and machinery are others. This book looks at yet another kind of technology: transportation.

Ancient Roots

Transportation is one of the oldest technologies. It involves the movement of people and goods from one place to another.

Phoenician boats, such as the one in this carving from the fourth century BCE, were the earliest vessels to sail the Mediterranean Sea.

People have used transportation technologies to escape enemies, send messages to one another, and reach new places to live. When we think of transportation, we often think of cars, trains, airplanes, trucks, and ships. But there is much more to this technology. Water pipes transport water from place to place. Electrical lines carry power across long distances. Fiber-optic cables move information around the world. Transportation also includes older technologies, such as maps, ports, lighthouses, and bridges.

Engineers and scientists rarely make completely new advances in transportation technology. Engineers might develop roads that last longer, wheels that turn faster, or longer bridges. But many times, these accomplishments improve on techniques developed by earlier peoples. For example, modern freeways and other roads have an arched shape. The sides slope down from the center. This allows water to drain off. The ancient Romans invented this design more than twenty-three hundred years ago.

Ancient cultures left us a rich legacy of transportation technology. How do we know so much about their technology? Archaeologists piece together clues to understand how ancient vehicles worked. They study the remains of ancient vehicles and try to piece them together or guess how each part worked. In some cases, ancient people left pictures, diagrams, and written descriptions of their technology. So even if a vehicle is gone, modern archaeologists can still learn a lot about it.

CHAPTER ONE

Transportation Basics

The first *Homo sapiens*, or modern humans, lived about 300,000 years ago. They were hunter-gatherers. They lived in small groups and got their food by hunting game, fishing, and gathering wild plants. When the food in one area was all used up, a group moved to a new place. Hunter-gatherers made tools from stone, wood, animal bones, plant fibers, and clay.

Hunter-gatherers traveled constantly. They followed herds of animals. They killed animals for meat, furs, bones, and other materials. Natural disasters such as droughts, wildfires, volcanic eruptions, and climate change also forced ancient people to move.

Speed was important. Hunters who killed an elk had to bring it back to their camp before other animals stole it.

Early peoples had few possessions, but they probably traveled with blankets and stone tools. People with the most efficient ways of carrying heavy loads were the most likely to survive.

Ancient Footwear

People walked before they used any transportation technology. But as ancient humans moved to more distant places, their feet needed help. Just try walking barefoot on the ground with sharp stones underneath. Ouch. To make walking easier, people invented foot coverings. Shoes and sandals enabled people to travel farther, faster, in colder weather, and over rougher terrain.

Ancient peoples in cold regions of Asia and Europe probably

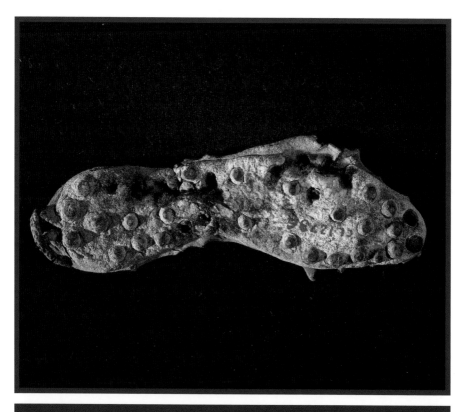

Spike-bottomed leather sandals, known as caligae, provided Roman soldiers not only with a better grip during battle, but also with the ability to injure an enemy with their feet.

made the first foot coverings. They probably used animal skins with fur or hair that protected feet against cold and snow. People quickly realized that the skins also made walking more comfortable.

Ancient peoples later developed many kinds of warm-weather footwear. Egyptian wall paintings show people wearing sandals with soles made from papyrus plants. People in ancient Japan wore shoes that looked like flip flops with carved wooden soles. They were fastened to the feet with vines or ropes. In the ancient Middle East, shoemakers added tough leather soles for rough terrain. Laces made from strips of leather held these shoes firmly in place.

Foot covering technology dates back to at least 7,000 BCE. The oldest known leather shoe was discovered in a cave in modern-day Armenia. It was made at least fifty-five hundred years ago. However, much of the world walked barefoot for many centuries. Like many new technologies, shoes were expensive. In many cultures, they were available only to soldiers or the rich.

The First Boats

Ancient peoples probably got the idea for boats from their environment. They probably noticed tree branches floating down rivers. After floods, they would have seen animals clinging to floating tree trunks. Eventually, people also clung to logs. They could have moved across lakes and ponds by kicking their feet and paddling with their hands. These simple floats were likely the first boats. Later, people began to tie logs together to make rafts. Rafts were better. They do not spin or tip over as easily. Rafts can also carry heavier loads.

A canoe made from a wooden frame covered in bark allowed passengers and their belongings to stay dry while traveling, hunting, and fishing.

Ancient people realized that it would be even better to sit inside a floating log. They used sharp stone tools or fire to hollow out logs and create dugout canoes. The remains of one dugout canoe, discovered in what is now the Netherlands, was built about eight thousand years ago. Scientists think it is the world's oldest boat. People sat in dugouts and paddled from one place to another. They also used them to hunt, fish, and carry cargo. Dugout canoes are still used throughout the world.

Tree bark provided material for boats that were lighter, faster, and easier to build. Ancient people built a wooden frame in the shape of a canoe. Then they attached big strips of

The Moving Force

Boats and other kinds of transportation need propulsion to move. Propulsion is the force that moves things. First came human propulsion with muscles moving legs as people walked. For boats, muscles were combined with paddles. Paddles are short poles flattened at one end. Pull a paddle back through the water, and the canoe moves forward.

That technology worked fine for rivers and small lakes. But putting boats on the ocean required new propulsion. Sails powered by wind and later steam engines powered by burning coal were the answer.

For other forms of transportation, the moving force came from horses, camels, elephants, and even dogs. Later on, propulsion came from other engines burning gasoline, diesel fuel, jet fuel, and rocket fuel. More and more cars and trucks use electric motors.

bark peeled from trees. Sticky sap from spruce and other trees served as waterproof glue to seal the strips.

The Algonquin people built some of the first birchbark canoes. They lived in what is now the northeastern United States and Canada more than eight thousand years ago.

Beasts of Burden

The hunter-gatherer lifestyle was common until about 10,000 BCE. Then people in the ancient Middle East began to settle down in permanent villages and farms. They grew grain, vegetables, and fruit. They domesticated wild animals.

Domesticating is similar to taming. Domesticated animals live among humans instead of in the wild. Ancient peoples trained dogs to pull travois, sledges, and other vehicles. Researchers have discovered the remains of domesticated dogs, some as old as ten thousand years, in China, Germany, and elsewhere.

People later used yokes to harness vehicles to larger animals, such as oxen and buffalo. With these stronger animals, people could move enormous loads over greater distances. People also used wild donkeys to pull their vehicles. Wild donkeys are related to horses. These animals once lived wild around the Mediterranean.

Domesticated donkeys are slower than horses but gentler and more sure-footed. Early traders used them as pack animals. People loaded cargo on the animals' backs for long trips. After the invention of the wheel, warriors used donkeys to pull two-wheeled wagons called chariots.

Ancient peoples also rode on camels and used them to carry goods. Camels also supplied travelers with milk. When camels died or were killed, people ate their meat. When camels shed their long hair every summer, people wove it into fabric.

Use of the camel was a great advance in the history of land transportation. Camels allowed people to develop trade routes across vast spaces, including deserts.

A Well-Trod Road

The first roads were paths of packed earth. Deer, buffalo, and other animals trampled them down as they repeatedly took the same route to watering spots. Hunters used these paths to track their prey and get their own water. Early peoples made roads in the same way—with their own feet.

In 1970 a laborer named Ray Sweet discovered the remains of an elevated walkway in southwestern England while digging in a peat bog. Archaeologists estimate that builders created the walkway in 3807 or 3806 BCE. The bog's soil partially preserved the walkway over time. The road is known as the Sweet Track. It measures about 9,843 feet (3,000 m) in length.

The Sweet Track is one of the oldest timber trackways in the British Isles. It provided travelers a dry passage over swampy, marshy terrain. That same terrain helped preserve the wood used to build the walkway more than six thousand years ago.

The Sweet Track was made of wooden planks and crisscrossing tree branches. The branches were hammered diagonally into the soft soil and extended above ground level to create a series of V shapes. Using stone tools, builders split planks from tree trunks. They laid the planks over the areas where the branches intersected. People walked along the elevated plank pathway, allowing them to traverse the low, swampy area more easily.

Skis and Sledges

Archaeologists long thought that early peoples used skis for winter travel in cold areas of Asia and Europe. Skis, made of long flat wooden boards, spread weight over a wide area and allow skiers to glide easily over snow. But wood rots quickly. As a result, archaeologists had no physical evidence of ancient skis. Then in 1964 Russian archaeologists discovered the remains of a ski preserved in a peat bog in northeastern Russia. Laboratory analysis of the wood indicated that the ski was made around 6000 BCE.

One of the oldest-known pictures of a skier is carved on a rock wall in Rødøy, Norway. The forty-five-hundred-year-old carving shows a skier using a single pole to push himself forward. The skis were probably 10 feet (3 m) long.

Early hunters most likely used skis to find game and to carry food back to their families. Warriors may also have used skis in winter battles.

The first sledges, or sleighs, were flat boards used to drag things over land. They marked a significant advance in people's ability to transport heavy loads. Sledges can be pulled over slick or uneven ground. The addition of ski-like runners

at the bottom of a sledge made it easier to pull heavy loads over snow and ice. Archaeologists believe that people used sledges as early as 3500 BCE.

Heavy Loads

Archaeologists believe that early hunters used a simple device called a yoke to transport heavy loads. A yoke was a pole or curved piece of wood. A hunter, for instance, could balance the pole over their shoulder with loads fastened on each end. Two hunters could also tie a large carcass onto a yoke and each carry one end.

The yoke led to the development of the travois. A travois consists of two long poles bound together at an angle. A platform often lays between the poles to support a load. The first travois may have been made from forked tree branches with a load placed on the forked portion. People pulled the other end of the branch by hand or perhaps fastened it to someone's waist. The loaded end dragged along the ground. This allowed people to carry heavier loads farther than ever before.

CHAPTER TWO
The Ancient Middle East

Around 6000 BCE, several cultures began to develop in the ancient Middle East—the region around the southern and eastern shores of the Mediterranean Sea. This region contains the Fertile Crescent, an arc of land extending from the eastern Mediterranean Sea to the Persian Gulf. Because the land was good for farming, people settled there in the first permanent villages. Some people settled between the Tigris and Euphrates Rivers in present-day Iraq, Syria, and Turkey. The Greeks later named the region Mesopotamia, which means "between rivers."

Sumer is the earliest known civilization. It arose sometime between 4500 and 4000 BCE in southern Mesopotamia. The Sumerians invented a system of writing called cuneiform. Their most important invention in transportation technology was the wheel. Thousands of years later, the Phoenicians built great port cities such as Sidon and Tyre. The Phoenicians established distant trading posts, including the famous city of Carthage in northern Africa. Other groups in Mesopotamia included the Babylonians and the Assyrians.

The Tigris River in western Asia has provided water and power for the Fertile Crescent for thousands of years. It has also provided a way for civilizations to travel and trade.

Rafts, Floats, and Riverboats

Around 2000 BCE, the Assyrians built the first inflatable rafts. These boats, called keleks, preceded modern inflatable rafts. Keleks were made from many sheepskins. People made them by sewing sheepskins together to form airtight bags. Then they inflated the skins like balloons. Next they attached the inflated skins to a frame of strong willow rods. A platform covered with reeds or moss sat atop the skins. Large keleks could contain up to twenty inflated sheepskins. Like modern rafts, keleks could bounce off rocks. They were less likely to break apart in rough water. That made them ideal for carrying passengers and goods safely through mountain streams.

The Assyrians also used inflated sheepskins as individual floats. Ancient wall carvings show people floating in the water on inflated skins. They probably used the floats for work and not play. It took a lot of time and effort to prepare a sheepskin with airtight seams. The floats probably were far too expensive to be used as toys. The carvings show people floating alongside keleks and helping steer the rafts.

The Assyrians also made another kind of boat from uninflated sheepskins. It was a circular riverboat for transporting cargo, soldiers, and civilians. Boatbuilders stretched the skins over a framework of willow branches or reeds. They sealed

This model shows two Assyrian men transporting cargo using a small kelek. These boats featured inflated animals skins and were used for thousands of years to travel on the Tigris and Euphrates Rivers.

the seams between skins with a naturally occurring sticky material called bitumen. It was like the sticky black material in modern asphalt.

Some boats could hold only one or two people. Others could carry heavy cargo. Ancient writers said that the biggest boats could carry five thousand talents. A talent is an ancient unit of weight. Five thousand talents weighed about 290,000 pounds (131,542 kg).

The Sail

Most early peoples used oars and paddles to power their boats. The Phoenicians were possibly the first people to realize the advantages of wind power over human power. Their ships were called gauloi, which means "round ship." Rigged with sails, gauloi began long sea voyages starting around 3000 BCE. Phoenician boatbuilders made sails from heavy cloth such as linen.

Gauloi were the first freighters, or large cargo ships. Gauloi could carry more goods than any earlier boat. The Phoenicians also used the sturdy gauloi as a warship.

Gauloi relied on a single large sail fixed in one position. It could not be raised or lowered in response to changing wind conditions like a modern sail. Gauli and vessels like them could make progress only when the wind blew in the right direction. Unfavorable winds and storms often disrupted ancient sea transport.

Gauloi also had oars. Sailors used them mainly to steer the ships as they entered or left harbors. In wartime, captains relied on sails as much as possible. They conserved the strength of the rowers for battle. But just before battle, sailors removed the sail and mast and left them on a nearby beach for safekeeping. Ancient warships often rammed one another. A collision could knock the mast off one or both vessels.

Horsepower

Ancient cave paintings and carvings engraved in animal tusks suggest that humans have known about horses for more than thirty thousand years. Early peoples probably regarded the animals as a food source, not as transportation. Cave paintings often show people hunting horses.

Sometime between 4000 and 3000 BCE, people in the

This relief from the Ruins of Persepolis in modern-day Iran shows people using domesticated livestock for work and transportation.

ancient Middle East tamed wild horses. They captured them, fed them, and tended to their illnesses and injuries. A small clay figurine found north of modern-day Damascus, Syria, depicts a domesticated horse. The figurine dates to about 2300 BCE. By this time, it would have been common to see a horse in captivity.

At first, people probably kept horses for meat, milk, and goods that could be made from horsehair and horsehide. Later, people used horses to carry packs on trade routes. Some experts also think that ancient people kept horses mainly to breed mules. A mule is the offspring of a female horse and a male donkey. Mules look a lot like horses but have larger ears, smaller hooves, and tufted tails. They are more reliable than horses on rocky or difficult ground.

Saddle Up!

Use of the horse for transportation was one of the most important advances in technology. It truly revolutionized life for ancient people. An average runner can jog at 6 miles per hour for a few hours. A horse can trot twice as fast and travel 100 miles in a single day. Horses were used to transport people and all kinds of goods, and for farming, hunting and recreation.

Early horses were small. Most horses probably measured about twelve hands in height at the shoulder. That's about 4 feet (1.2 m). The width of an average adult human hand is the standard measure of horse height —about 4 inches (10 cm).

Eventually early peoples began to breed horses for greater size. They mated their largest horses together to produce a larger foal. Horseback riding became more practical as horses grew larger and stronger. Experts aren't sure when horse breeding began. But horseback riding became popular in the ancient Middle East after around 2000 BCE.

The Wheel

No other technology can match the wheel in its simplicity and its impact on society. Wheeled vehicles can move quickly and efficiently. Wheels provide the basis for gears, pulleys, and other machines.

The oldest known depiction of a wheel appears on a clay tablet from about 3500 BCE. It is the same Mesopotamian tablet on which a picture of an ancient sledge appears.

People did not invent the first wheel for transportation. Archaeologists think the first wheels were potter's wheels. These wooden disks spun horizontally. People placed lumps of clay on them and spun them, using their hands to shape the clay into round vessels. Experts are not certain when or how the potter's wheel became a cart wheel. Perhaps carpenters moved newly completed potter's wheels by rolling them. Perhaps children rolled the wheels as toys. Then someone attached them to axles and put a sledge on top.

The wheel was most likely invented only once, in Mesopotamia, though there is some evidence that ancient Americans knew about wheels too. It quickly spread from Mesopotamia to other civilizations in Asia, Africa, and Europe. In Europe researchers have found the remains of four-wheeled, animal-drawn wagons that may be as old as five thousand years. Archaeologists have also found evidence of wheel use in India just after 3500 BCE and in Egypt by 2500 BCE.

People eventually learned to reduce the weight of the three-part wheel by carving out inner sections of the disk. Inventors in Mesopotamia developed the spoked wheel around 2000 BCE. Spokes are thin bars connecting a wheel's outer rim and inner hub. Spoked wheels were much lighter than solid wheels and moved faster. The use of spokes quickly spread beyond the Middle East.

By 1400 BCE, Egyptian woodworkers were making strong, light wheels by putting together separate rims, spokes, and hubs. Woodworkers nailed strips of copper or bronze to the outside of the wheels to reduce wear. The Egyptians first used these improved wheels on expensive racing and war chariots.

Some cultures tried the wheel and found it unsuitable. People in parts of Asia and the Middle East preferred camels to wheeled carts. Camels were more efficient for travel over desert sands and rough terrain.

The Mahawi

In the Arabian Peninsula, camels were used for transportation instead of horses. This desert land included modern-day Saudi Arabia, Kuwait, and Iraq. The people there domesticated camels around four thousand years ago. Camels were perfect for transportation in this desert land. Camels can go for weeks without water and months without food. They carry heavier loads than horses. But people could not use camels for transportation until the invention of the mahawi. *Mahawi* means "saddle" in the Arabic language. A camel saddle flattened out the area around the animal's hump. It consisted of a leather-covered wooden seat and wooden frame that fit over the hump.

CHAPTER THREE
Ancient Egypt

Around 8000 BCE, northern Africa's wet climate became drier. Hunter-gatherers in the area began to move east, toward the Nile River in Egypt.

By about 7000 BCE, people had built farming settlements along the river. The Nile flooded its banks every July. The floodwater soaked the soil and deposited fertile silt similar to mud on the surrounding land. Early Egyptian farmers grew an abundance of wheat, barley, vegetables, and fruits.

The Nile flows for 4,145 miles (6,671 km), making it one of the longest rivers in the world. It was a natural pathway for transporting goods and people. Traders floated with the northern current in reed ships. They deposited their cargoes at Egyptian cities such as Thebes, Memphis, and Giza. Then they sailed and rowed south against the current back to home ports. From the mouth of the Nile, Egyptian merchants established trading routes to Asia, Greece, and other places.

The Nile River is frequently associated with Egypt, but its banks include ten other countries, including Tanzania, the Democratic Republic of the Congo, and Kenya.

Navigating the Nile

The first Egyptian boats were rafts made from tightly woven papyrus reeds. Boaters used poles to guide the rafts through shallow water. A wall painting completed around 3500 BCE shows crews of rowers in papyrus boats. One crew member uses a steering paddle to guide each boat.

Egyptian boat makers also attached a mast and square sail to their vessels around 350 BCE. The sail was not stuck in a fixed position as it was on Phoenician ships. Instead, the sail could be raised or lowered as needed. Ships traveling south

This wall painting depicts rowing crews steering a papyrus boat along the Nile River.

on the Nile required a sail. Luckily for the sailors, winds in Egypt often blow in from the north. When traveling north, sailors lowered the sail and ran with the current. The ships also had oars for power in calm weather and for maneuvering near docks. Passengers, crew, and cargo rode on deck under cloth shelters. Some Egyptian ships also had cabins beneath the deck for passengers, with shades that rolled up and down.

Seafaring Vessels

The Egyptians built larger boats to navigate trade routes on the Mediterranean Sea. Some of these vessels were 180 feet (55 m) long and 60 feet (18 m) wide. In 1954 an Egyptian archaeologist found the remains of a magnificent ship buried in a sandpit, under heavy stone slabs, near the Great Pyramid of Giza. The Great Pyramid is the tomb of Khufu, an Egyptian pharaoh who lived around 2600 BCE. It is the largest of several pyramids on the outskirts of Cairo, Egypt.

The ship found buried nearby was in 1,224 separate pieces. Experts spent more than a decade carefully putting the ship back together. The reconstructed vessel was more than 143 feet (44 m) long. It is possible that no one ever actually sailed on the ship. The vessel contained oars but was not watertight. Researchers believe the ship was a ceremonial barge.

Ancient Egyptians believed in life after death. To ensure a person's well-being in the afterlife, Egyptians carefully preserved the person's body. They also buried the person with items that would reflect their mortal life. Khufu's barge was most likely meant to assist him on his journey through the afterlife.

Egyptian Maps

Ancient Egyptians carved maps in stone, drew maps on papyrus scrolls, and painted maps on pottery and tomb walls. With a single known exception, however, these maps were not intended to help people find their way from one location to another. Instead, the maps were religious and symbolic documents. Some showed secret routes to the afterlife. Others illustrated astronomers' concepts of the universe, including the realms of Egyptian gods and goddesses.

The modern Suez Canal, shown here, was completed in 1869 and is integral to contemporary commerce.

Archaeologists have also found model boats in the tombs of other Egyptian leaders. Some of the boats have canopies, sails, and even model rowers.

The Ancient Suez Canal

The Suez Canal, a modern, human-made Egyptian waterway, gives ships a shortcut from the Mediterranean Sea to the Red Sea. What would travel be like without this 101-mile (162-km) channel? Container ships, oil tankers, cruise ships, and warships traveling east from Europe would have to sail around the tip of Africa to reach ports in the Indian Ocean. The canal, finished in 1869, reduces the distance between Europe and Asia by 4,200 miles (7,000 km).

But early peoples built another Suez Canal more than three thousand years earlier. In the thirteenth century BCE, ancient Egyptian engineers dug a canal that also allowed ships to pass directly from the Mediterranean Sea to the Red Sea. It followed a different route than the modern Suez Canal. It linked a branch of the Nile River north of Cairo with the Red Sea. Historians believe the project originated either with Seti I, a pharaoh who reigned from about 1290 to 1279 BCE, or with Ramesses II, who ruled from 1279 to 1213 BCE.

The early canal gradually became less useful. It was eventually filled in by blowing sand and forgotten. But

"I ordered that this canal be dug from the river which is called Nile, which flows in Egypt, to the sea which goes from Persia. Then the canal was dug as I commanded, and ships sailed from Egypt through this canal to Persia, according to my will."

—Persian king Darius I, from a pillar celebrating the canal's construction, fifth century BCE.

several centuries later, other Egyptian leaders recognized the benefits of a passage between the Nile and the Red Sea.

Many historians believe that construction of yet another canal began under Necho II, who ruled Egypt from 610 to 595 BCE. The project stalled following Necho's death. Later, King Darius I of Persia, who lived from 550 to 486 BCE, ruled Egypt. He also ordered the building of a waterway to the Red Sea. Unlike the rulers before him, he saw the canal completed in his lifetime. Darius was very proud of the achievement. He boasted about it through carved messages on granite pillars along the waterway.

Darius's engineers may have been aware of the earlier waterway connecting the Mediterranean Sea and the Red Sea. Some visible remains of the first Suez Canal likely survived until Darius's reign. Some archaeologists think the engineers may have saved unnecessary labor by repairing segments of the earlier canal whenever possible.

Sledges and Paved Roads

Some of the stones used to build Egypt's pyramids, sculptures, and other monuments weigh more than 4,000 pounds (1,814 kg). Archaeologists believe sledges played a big role in moving these heavy blocks. People transported stones on sledges from rock quarries to the Nile and onto barges and from the barges to building sites. Workers also used sledges to move stones up temporary earthen ramps and into position at pyramids.

Sometimes one form of technology creates the need for another. Archaeologists believe that such a link exists between sledges and paved roads. Sledges were not always an effective way to carry blocks of stone across the desert. Occasionally, heavy loads sank into the sand, so the Egyptians decided to pave over it.

The remains of one paved road extend about 7.5 miles (12 km) through the desert southwest of Cairo. Discovered by the US Geological Survey in 1994, the path is thought to be the oldest paved road in the world. Artifacts found along the road date between 2600 and 2134 BCE. The road had an average width of 6.5 feet (2 m) and was made from slabs of sandstone and limestone laid end to end.

Ancient Egyptians built the road to haul stones on sledges from a rock quarry to a dock at ancient Lake Moeris near the Nile River. Workers loaded stones onto barges and floated them through a natural canal connecting the lake to the Nile. The barges then floated downriver to pyramid sites.

Ancient Egyptian workers may have used sledges like the one shown here to drag stones up ramps during the construction of the pyramids.

CHAPTER FOUR
Ancient China

The first large Chinese society emerged between 5000 and 3000 BCE in the Yellow River valley of northern China. There, early peoples settled into small farming villages. The river provided water for drinking, irrigation, fishing, and transportation. When the river flooded the land, it left behind layers of rich soil for farming.

China has many waterways, but few are connected to one another naturally. So the ancient Chinese dug numerous canals. They created a watery transportation network that linked rivers from many parts of China.

Amazing Canal Builders

Eastern China is home to the world's largest canal, the Grand Canal. The Grand Canal covers nearly 1,120 miles (1,800 km) from north to south. It provides passage between the modern Chinese cities of Beijing and Hangzhou. The construction of the Grand Canal began around 486 BCE. Work on the canal continued for more than one hundred years.

TRANSPORTATION THROUGH THE AGES

China's Yellow River is considered the cradle of Chinese civilization. The "mother river of China" was central to the country's politics, economy, culture, and technological development for more than 3,000 years.

In one sense, construction of the Grand Canal started even earlier. A smaller canal, the Hong Gou (Canal of Flying Geese), already linked China's Yellow River to several other rivers throughout the country. The northernmost part of the Grand Canal later incorporated a section of the Hong Gou. Researchers are unsure when the Hong Gou was first constructed. It may have existed in some form as early as the sixth century BCE.

The Marvelous Junk

The ancient Chinese sailed down canals in a type of ship that came to be known as a junk. Junks were boxy and ungainly. They had a flat bottom, a high stern (rear), and a low bow (front).

The junk had no keel and no sternpost. On most boats, keels act like a backbone and help hold everything together. Sternposts help support other parts of a boat's back end. Even without these parts, junks were among the strongest and most seaworthy vessels ever designed.

The junk's high stern allowed the deck to stay dry when waves crashed from behind. The design also assured that the ship would safely turn with its bow to the wind when anchored. Its flat bottom allowed safe sailing through shallow water and easy beaching onshore.

Junk boats were the first ships built with stern-mounted rudders, which allowed for easier steering. These rudders would be adopted by other civilizations centuries later and are still used today.

A rudder, or heavy steering oar, made up for the lack of a keel. The rudder was mounted in a watertight space. It extended through the boat's deck and hull (outer body). The rudder could be raised in shallow water to prevent damage and lowered again with ease. Sails were made of bamboo mats or linen fabric. Crew members could open and close them quickly with changing wind conditions.

A major advantage of the junk's boxy design was the exceptionally strong hull. Bulkheads ran lengthwise and crosswise inside the hull. They divided the hull into twelve or more watertight compartments. Bulkheads acted as barriers to incoming seawater. The compartments limited flooding if the ship struck rock or was damaged in battle. A hole in the hull might flood one compartment, but it probably would not sink the entire ship.

The Wooden Ox

The ancient Chinese also innovated a form of land transportation. Chinese inventors devised a simple yet ingenious tool for moving heavy loads called the wooden ox. Their device consisted of a wooden frame, a single wheel, and two handles. We know it as the wheelbarrow.

With the wheelbarrow, one person could carry a load that had previously required two or three people. One soldier with a wheelbarrow could carry enough food to supply four others for up to three months. Ancient Chinese wheelbarrows had one wheel in the middle of a cart, directly under the load. With this arrangement, the pusher's main work involved balancing and steering.

The wheelbarrow was probably in use by 206 BCE.

How the Junk Got Its Name

The name *junk* has nothing to do with garbage. People from the Southeast Asian island of Java used the term *jong* to refer to all sailing vessels. This included the bulky Chinese ships that sometimes visited Java's shores.

In the seventeenth century, Portuguese and Dutch travelers began visiting Java. These travelers began using the Javanese term for boat. But the European sailors pronounced it "junco." English speakers adopted the word junk as a term for Chinese ships after hearing the Portuguese and the Dutch use similar terms.

Outside of battle, the Chinese used wheelbarrows to transport people and goods, such as rice and vegetables. Some later versions of wheelbarrows could hold several passengers.

The Silk Road

The Han dynasty led China from 206 BCE to 200 CE. China underwent great economic growth during this period. Chinese merchants drove groups of camels from cities along the Yellow River through central Asia to the Middle East. These merchants traded jade and bronze for rugs, horses, glass, and other products. But the main Chinese export was silk, a soft, shimmery fabric. So much silk traveled over this route from China to the Middle East that it became known as the Silk Road.

Few merchants made the entire trip. The Silk Road extended thousands of miles over land from Chang'an in east

The Silk Road trade routes across Asia totaled more than 4,000 miles (6,437 kilometers). The exchanges of products, information, and ideas that took place along the Silk Road led to some of history's most significant technological developments.

central China through modern Syria to the eastern coast of the Mediterranean. Traders continued by sea to Rome and Venice. Goods typically changed hands many times along the road.

The Silk Road came to serve as an ancient technological superhighway. Merchants exchanged information about new ideas and innovations. For instance, hitching horses one behind the other saved space on narrow roads. The Chinese began this practice and passed it on to people in the Middle East and Europe.

CHAPTER FIVE
Ancient India

People in western India began settling into villages around 4000 BCE. Within one thousand years, one of the world's greatest civilizations had emerged in this region. It covered an area of around 300,000 square miles (777,000 sq km) in modern-day Pakistan and India. It is called the Indus Valley Civilization because it developed along the Indus River.

About 1700 BCE, people began to leave the Indus Valley. Experts believe that floods or changing river patterns may have caused the end of the Indus Valley Civilization.

Two hundred years later, the Aryans invaded India. The Aryans were probably a warlike Indo-Iranian people from central Asia, though some historians believe they came from India itself. Aryan invaders spread throughout northern India and settled into villages. Around 518 BCE, warriors from Persia took control of northwestern India, including parts of modern-day Pakistan. Around 324 BCE, a new empire formed. Chandragupta Maurya, a ruler descended from India's central Asian conquerors, united all of northern India.

Some of the biggest ancient civilizations in the world were located along the Indus River. The river remains an important source of water, irrigation, and industry for modern-day Pakistan and India.

The Mauryan Empire controlled the north for about one hundred years. It dissolved after the death of Chandragupta's grandson Ashoka. But another empire, the Gupta Empire, took the place of the Mauryans. Throughout these many changes, people from central Asia continued coming to India.

Elephant Power

For travel, trade, warfare, and construction work, ancient Indians used the world's biggest and most powerful beast of burden—the elephant. Male Indian elephants grow to between

An adult Indian elephant can carry around 2,000 pounds (907 kg). Elephants also have good stamina and can move at a steady pace while carrying riders or cargo, so this made them a good option for transportation.

9 and 10 feet (2.7 to 3 m) in height and can weigh up to 8,000 pounds (3,600 kg). A fully grown female Indian elephant stands about 1 foot (0.3 m) shorter and weighs several hundred pounds less. Although male elephants are more powerful than females, workers used female elephants more often for transportation because they were easier to work with.

Ancient Indians knew that elephants were intelligent and could be trained to perform certain tasks. They captured elephant calves in the wild and assigned each calf a keeper. An elephant's keeper stayed with the animal for life.

Elephants transported rulers and other wealthy people on saddles or in small, covered compartments. They also carried merchandise along trade routes. Elephants were ideal for logging in jungles because of their massive size. They could smash their way through heavy undergrowth while carrying logs with their powerful trunks. Some modern logging operations in India still use elephants.

Ancient Indians also used elephants in warfare. Soldiers rode on saddles fastened around the animals' necks. In wartime, elephants even wore heavy leather armor for protection.

Scholars are not sure when the ancient Indians first began to use elephants for combat. A battle between the forces of Macedonian general and king Alexander the Great and King Porus of Paurava (a kingdom in the Punjab region of India and Pakistan) marks one of the earliest recorded instances of elephant warfare. Alexander encountered two hundred of these fighting animals when he and his army of 120,000 soldiers invaded Paurava in 326 BCE.

The Big-Toe Stirrup

Ancient Indians also fought on horseback. Indian riders introduced a major advance in warfare and transportation with the development of a simple device: the stirrup. A stirrup is a support for a rider's foot that hangs down from each side of a saddle.

Archaeologists have examined depictions of horses on ancient statues, coins, and other artifacts. These artifacts

Stirrups helped riders mount their horses, but they also gave them more stability while riding. This was especially important during travel on rough terrain, or during battle when a soldier might get knocked to the ground.

show that for thousands of years, most early peoples did not use stirrups. Evidence suggests that ancient Indian riders introduced the first stirrups between 300 and 200 BCE.

The stirrup is so simple that some people might not even regard it as technology. But the stirrup was revolutionary. Stirrups made horses more accessible. Without stirrups, riders had to leap onto horses, and only people in top physical condition could jump so high.

Merchants who traveled the Silk Road carried stirrup technology from India to China and eventually from India to Europe. King Charles Martel, who ruled the area that eventually became Germany and Belgium, adopted the stirrup in the eighth century CE. Stirrups gave Charles's soldiers an advantage in warfare.

Ancient Indian Boating

The people of ancient India used a wide variety of seacraft. The landscape along India's coast changes from region to region. So did the designs of ancient Indian boats. On the central west coast, people used boats such as dugout canoes. Later, outriggers were common. These ships have beams extending over the side of the boat. This makes the boat more stable and less bouncy.

People on India's east coast also used dugout canoes. They also used masula, boats with planks and frames bound together by stiff rope. Masula were typically used for fishing and travel to nearby areas. But plank boats could not dock as easily upon east India's southern coastline because of the area's harsh breaking waves. Log rafts called catamarans were more practical for sailing in the southeast. Travelers in catamarans could safely cross the dangerous surf and then take their boats apart to dry on sandy shores. Archaeologists believe a fishing community in the modern Indian state of Tamil Nadu developed the catamaran sometime before 500 CE.

Catamarans have two hulls beneath a single deck. They are now used all around the world.

CHAPTER SIX
The Ancient Americas

The first people in North America probably arrived about thirty thousand years ago. That's about fifteen thousand years earlier than many historians once thought. They came from Siberia in modern-day Russia. One theory claimed that humans walked across a land bridge that once linked Siberia and modern-day Alaska. Ocean levels were lower then. Another theory suggests that ancient peoples sailed from Siberia, staying close to the coast of the Pacific Ocean. After sailing over open stretches of water, they camped on the shore. They needed to rest and get food and fresh water. No matter how they arrived, these newcomers were hunter-gatherers. They probably followed herds of wooly mammoths and other Ice Age animals deeper into North America.

Ancient Americans slowly moved south through modern-day Canada. They reached the American Great Plains, modern-day Mexico, and Central America. Scientists once thought that humans arrived at the tip of South America about twelve thousand years ago. But new evidence suggests

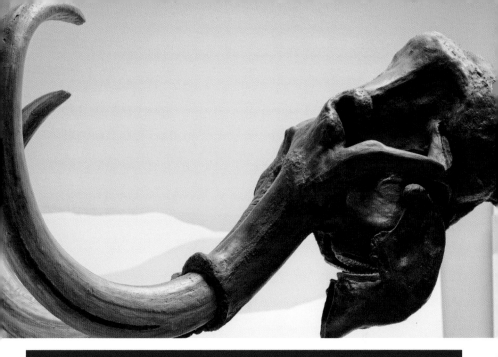

Woolly mammoths lived in the northern tundra of North America, Asia, and Europe until about 10,000 years ago.

that it happened at least three thousand years earlier.

Ancient North America

Few artifacts and no written records of this group's transportation technology exist. Archaeologists assume that these Paleo-Indians in North America relied on foot coverings, yokes, and other technologies similar to those used by hunter-gatherers in Eurasia and elsewhere. But it is known that Indigenous peoples across the Great Plains relied on the travois.

The travois was a wooden frame made of two long poles with a net or wooden platform between them for carrying gear. It helped people deal with the Great Plains' varied landscapes and sometimes harsh weather. A traveler could pull cargo over snow or soil and through prairies or forests. Indigenous Americans such as the Cheyenne and the Lakota peoples even used the travois in the nineteenth century CE.

For hundreds or even thousands of years, the early peoples of North America harnessed the travois to domesticated dogs. In the sixteenth century, Spanish explorers began to arrive in the Americas. The Spanish brought with them a more powerful load-bearing animal: the horse. Indigenous Americans in the Great Plains soon began harnessing travois to horses as well. Peoples throughout North America also quickly adopted the practice of riding on horseback. Riding horses allowed Indigenous Americans to be more effective in both hunting and combat.

An early photograph shows Indigenous Americans using a travois to pull passengers and cargo behind a horse.

Bridges of the Inca

The Inca lived throughout much of South America in the fifteenth and sixteenth centuries. The Inca Empire included parts of present-day Colombia, Ecuador, Peru, Chile, Bolivia, and Argentina. A vast network of roads and bridges extended throughout the Inca's massive territory. In certain places, Inca bridges spanned vast river gorges. Some of these bridges were 150 feet (46 m) long or longer.

Inca builders began constructing a bridge by weaving long ropes out of plant fibers. Then they braided many ropes together to make thick cables. Five cables formed the framework of the bridge. Two of these cables were handrails. Three other cables served as the bridge floor. Bridge builders attached the five cables to stone supports on both sides of the gorge.

Builders attached pieces of wood to the floor cables to create a solid surface for walking. In some cases, they tied wood and branches to the side cables to create walls. Inca bridges were sturdy but flexible. They swayed in the fierce winds that blew through river gorges, but they supported the weight of the people and animals that moved across them.

The Q'eswachaka bridge in the Peruvian Andes is the last-remaining Incan suspension bridge.

While modern snowshoes are made from different materials, they do not look much different from the earliest models used by Indigenous people in North America more than 1,000 years ago.

The Assiniboine and other Indigenous American groups that lived in snowy regions used snowshoes to move quickly during hunts or long walks. Early snowshoes typically had a wooden frame with lacings made from animal hide. These shoes spread out weight across a wide surface like skis do and kept hunters' feet from sinking into snow.

Canoes and More

Ancient Americans used canoes to travel on North America's rivers and lakes. Archaeologists have found remains of these canoes in the northeast United States dating from six thousand years ago.

Different varieties of canoes were popular in different regions. Many peoples east of the Great Plains relied on lightweight bark canoes. Groups in southeastern North America traveled by dugout canoe as well. Dugout canoes were also common on the West Coast. Peoples in the Pacific Northwest created huge dugout boats from cedar and redwood trees. Some of these canoes measured more than 60 feet (18 m) in length.

In certain areas, Indigenous Americans used animal skins as a boatbuilding material. Animal skin kept water from leaking into the boat, and it was a more flexible building material than wood. Peoples of the Great Plains created small bull boats by stretching buffalo skin over rounded wooden frames. The ancient Inuit of modern-day northern Canada built similar boats with sealskin and walrus skin.

Mesoamerica

Many societies emerged in present-day Mexico and Central America. Historians use the term Mesoamerica to describe this area and its cultures prior to the arrival of European explorers and settlers in the sixteenth century. Researchers have found few written records from Mesoamerica. Much of what we know about Mesoamerican transportation technology comes from archaeology or the written accounts of the Spanish, who arrived in 1519.

The Mesoamericans never harnessed beasts of burden. Although cultures such as the Maya may have domesticated deer for use as a food source, they did not use them as draft animals. Nor did Mesoamericans rely on the wheel for transportation. Archaeologists know that some Mesoamericans knew how to construct wheels, because they have found clay toys with wheels and axles in ancient Maya ruins. But much of the terrain in what is now Mexico and elsewhere in the region wasn't suitable for full-scale wheeled vehicles. Many Mesoamerican settlements were in rugged upland regions and in tropical rain forests. Without land that was relatively flat, dry, and firm, wheeled crafts were not practical for trade or warfare.

Maya Ports and Trade

The Maya emerged around 2500 BCE. They developed a powerful empire in modern-day southern Mexico, Guatemala, Belize, El Salvador, and Honduras. The Maya built cities with paved streets. They developed a written language and made accurate observations about the movement of the sun, the moon, the stars, and the planets. The Maya are also one of the first known cultures to understand the mathematical concept of zero. Maya civilization peaked between 300 and 700 CE and then declined for unknown reasons.

The remains of Maya ports, including one on the island of Cerritos off the northern coast of the Yucatán Peninsula in Mexico, have given archaeologists clues about Maya sea travel. The port facilities, used between 300 BCE and 300 CE, included piers, docks, and an artificial canal. A seawall more than 1,000 feet (305 m) long protected boats in the harbor. Maya merchants probably brought canoes full of salt, fish, and other goods to the port for trading. But many questions remain about Maya transportation. Archaeologists don't know how the Maya transported food from farms to large urban areas or what vehicles they used.

The Olmec

The Olmec people lived in southern parts of Mexico between 1200 and 400 BCE. Among the Olmecs' best-known

Tikal, located in northern Guatemala, is one of the largest and most important Maya archeological sites in the world. The ruins at Tikal include Maya art and writing, temples, residences, and even courts where ancient ball games were played.

achievements is the carving and moving of huge stone heads. The heads are cube-shaped, with smooth, rounded corners and flat faces in front. They were most likely designed to honor Olmec rulers. Some of these heads stand as tall as 9 feet (2.7 m). Most weigh 8 to 12 tons (7.25 to 10.9 t). Some weigh almost 50 tons (45 t). Historians know of seventeen stone heads, most of them at a site called San Lorenzo in southern Mexico.

Olmec sculptors carved the heads out of a volcanic rock called basalt. This rock comes from mountains more than 40 miles (64 km) away from San Lorenzo. Researchers are not sure how the Olmec managed to move such heavy objects. It's possible that the Olmec relied on sledges. If so, large groups of workers probably pulled the sledges over several months.

CHAPTER SEVEN
Ancient Greece

Geography often plays a role in the development of technology. Greece is a rugged land along the Mediterranean Sea. Ancient Greek farmers grew grapes, olives, and other fruits. But their farms were small. The Greeks had to look beyond their borders for a greater supply of food. Almost everywhere they looked, they saw ocean.

For this reason, the ancient Greeks excelled at shipbuilding, mapmaking, seafaring, trading, and naval warfare. The ancient Greeks' most important contributions to transportation technology involved the sea.

Beacons for Mariners

Lighthouses are beacons that guide sailors into harbors and warn of rocky shorelines that could sink a ship. Historians are unsure who constructed the first lighthouse, but it might have been the ancient Greeks. Some sources say that Lesches,

The Pharos of Alexandria is the first known lighthouse in history. Its light came from an open fire in the structure's topmost tower.

a legendary Greek poet, described a lighthouse as early as 660 BCE. But Lesches' works were lost and are unavailable to modern readers.

The most famous ancient lighthouse was the Pharos of Alexandria. It was built on a rocky island (also named Pharos) off the northern coast of Egypt in the Mediterranean Sea. The Pharos stood near the grand ancient city of Alexandria. Alexander the Great founded this city in 332 BCE. It became a cultural center for the ancient Greeks.

Ptolemy II governed Egypt from 283 to 246 BCE. Around 280 BCE, he ordered the construction of the Pharos. It was an important part of his plan to revitalize Egypt's economy by increasing trade with other countries. Greek

The Olympius, shown here, was completed in 1987 and is a replica of an ancient Athenian trireme. The vessel's builders used historical accounts, archeological findings, Greek literature, and ancient artwork to construct the boat.

architect Sostratus designed the structure. Workers completed the lighthouse in 247 BCE. The light guided cargo-laden merchant ships through the harbor of Alexandria.

An earthquake destroyed the lighthouse in the fourteenth century CE, so there is little accurate information about its construction. Some accounts indicate that the Pharos towered to a height of 600 feet (183 m)—as high as a sixty-story skyscraper. Others put the height at 350 feet (107 m). It was built of stone, with a square base, an octagonal midsection, and a round upper tower. A light in the tower burned so brightly that sailors reportedly could see it from 30 miles (48 km) away. Experts are unsure what materials lighthouse tenders burned in the lighthouse, but wood is the most likely answer.

The tower became so famous that *pharos* came to mean "lighthouse" in Greek and many other languages. The word is *faro* in Italian and *phare* in French. People who study lighthouse construction are called pharologists.

Triremes

The standard battleship in ancient Greece was a swift boat called the trireme. The trireme was equipped with a heavy battering ram in the front for sinking enemy ships. Once a trireme had rammed an enemy ship, sailors boarded the ship and attacked their rivals hand to hand or with swords. A typical trireme was about 140 feet (43 m) long and 20 feet (6 m) wide.

The word *trireme* comes from the Latin *triremis*, which means "having three oars to each bench." The vessels were outfitted with three decks of rowers. Thirty-one rowers typically occupied the top bank, with twenty-seven in each lower bank.

"[W]hat a size that ship was! 180 feet [55 m] long . . . and something over a quarter of that in width; and from deck to keep, the maximum depth, through the hold, 44 feet [13 m] . . . . The crew was like a small army."

—Lucian, Greek writer, on the freighter Isis, a 1,228-ton (1,114-metric-ton) ship, second century CE

Triremes evolved from the Phoenician bireme, an earlier, smaller vessel. It had two decks of rowers. According to the ancient Greek historian Thucydides, the people of the Greek city-state Corinth designed the first trireme around the seventh century BCE. Triremes gradually evolved into bigger battleships. According to legend, the last of these giant vessels seated thousands of rowers, with up to sixteen rowers pulling each huge oar.

Ancient Freighters

Alexandria was an important ancient trade center. Hundreds of merchant ships sailed trade routes to and from the city at the mouth of the Nile. The ships were laden with wine, olive oil, corn, wheat, fruit, timber, fabrics, dyes, hides, live animals, and a tremendous assortment of other goods.

Shipping costs were determined by the same factors twenty-three hundred years ago as they are in modern times. A key factor was the amount of cargo on a ship. Big ships transporting lots of cargo were more cost-effective than multiple smaller ships. Most Greek cargo ships could hold 150 tons (136 t) of freight. The standard Greek grain ship carried 340 tons (308 t). Some ships carried even more. By contrast, caravels—the most advanced ships built in fifteenth-century Spain and Portugal—held only about 125 tons (113 t).

Greek ships were built to carry a lot of cargo and withstand storms, but they were not necessarily built for speed. Even with favorable winds billowing their sails, most Greek freighters could travel at only about 6 knots—about 7 miles (11 km) per hour.

Proving a Round Earth

The Babylonians of Mesopotamia were great mapmakers. Over time, Babylonians introduced valuable map elements such as scales that related distance on a map to actual distances on Earth. From that base of knowledge, the Greeks made several technological leaps in mapping.

Most historians are convinced that Greek scholars were the first to realize that Earth is round rather than flat. Some trace the idea of a round Earth to Pythagoras, a Greek mathematician who lived from 580 to 500 BCE. Others think the idea originated with Parmenides, a Greek philosopher born around 515 BCE. In approximately 350 BCE, the Greek philosopher Aristotle developed six arguments for a round Earth. He noted, for instance, that travelers saw different constellations depending on where they were stationed. On a flat Earth, travelers would have seen the same constellations as they moved from place to place.

This map, drawn by Greek geographer, astronomer, and mathematician Ptolemy, was the first to use latitude and longitude lines, which indicate a curvature rather than a completely flat surface.

CHAPTER EIGHT

Ancient Rome

A ncient Rome was a great military power of the ancient world. From their base in present-day Italy, the Romans conquered many other countries and developed an empire that, at the height of its power, stretched through much of Europe, northern Africa, and parts of the Middle East.

To maintain this enormous empire, the Roman military needed a fast, reliable way to transport armies, supplies, and messages to distant regions. To fill that need, Rome built the ancient world's greatest highway system.

Roads Built to Last

The most durable Roman roads were made of layers of packed earth, stone blocks, sand, and other materials. Some roads were 5 feet (1.5 m) thick. They were paved with blocks of cut stone or with rocks mixed with cementlike material.

Roads through rainy areas had an arched surface that was higher in the center than at the sides. This shape allowed

Some Roman bridges, like the one depicted in this carving, were so well-constructed that they are still in use.

water to drain off the surface, so it would not soak into the road and damage it. (Many roads still have this design.) Most Roman roads had curbstones and drainage ditches at the sides. Stretches of road through towns had elevated sidewalks, so pedestrians could walk at a safe distance from draft animals and wheeled carts.

Many ancient civilizations, including the Mesopotamians, Egyptians, Indians, Chinese, and Greeks, built paved roads for the military. But none matched the system of roads begun in 312 BCE by the Roman politician Appius Claudius Caecus.

Appius Claudius's system included more than three hundred seventy major roads. The system extended across about 50,000 miles (80,467 km). It connected all the large towns of the Roman territories—from Greece to Spain to

"Appia teritur regina longarum viarum [The Appian Way is commonly said to be the queen of the long roads]."

—Publius Papinius Statius, Roman writer, Silvae, first century CE

Scotland. At every 1,000 paces (about 0.9 miles, or 1.5 km), markers along the roads told troops how far they had traveled.

The oldest and most famous Roman road was the Via Appia, or Appian Way. It went south from the Servian Wall in the city of Rome to the city of Capua in southern Italy. The road was more than 350 miles (563 km) long and 35 feet (11 m) wide.

Like many other Roman roads, the Appian Way was built as straight as possible. Although a straight line is the shortest distance between two towns, straight lines were an important aspect of Roman road design for another reason. Roman wagons had fixed axles. They could not move to steer the vehicle. Wagons could only travel straight, so roads had to be straight as well. To get a wagon off a road, workers had to inch it to the curb with huge pry bars.

Roman Travel Guides

Ancient Roman travelers used guides called *itineraria* (from the Latin word *itinerari*, meaning "to travel"). They were similar to modern-day packets of maps and travel brochures. Itineraria were written on parchment or papyrus. The guides showed the location of famous tombs and other sightseeing attractions, as well as roadhouses, bridges, rivers, and other features along roads. Itineraria sometimes mentioned areas of construction. They mainly focused on problems of greater concern to ancient travelers, such as hungry wolves on a path.

Experts believe that the master source for many itineraria may have been the Tabula Peutingeriana, or Peutinger Table. This parchment scroll showed all the roads of the Roman Empire, from the Middle East to Britain. The table showed the location of roadhouses and bathhouses. It listed distances and the most efficient routes between towns. The Peutinger Table in turn probably was based on a map of the world drawn by Marcus Agrippa, a Roman general who lived from 63 to 12 BCE.

Warships

Rome controlled the Mediterranean Sea for centuries. It built many warships to maintain its power. Some ships had catapults

Ancient Traffic Laws

Even in ancient times, roads had traffic jams, especially in the city of Rome. At times, oxcarts, chariots, handcarts, mounted horses, and farm wagons were barely able to move along the congested roads. The Roman Senate enacted traffic laws. It set up stop signs, one-way streets, and parking places. But these laws didn't solve the problem. Finally, ruler Julius Caesar, who lived from about 100 to 44 BCE, enacted a stricter traffic law. It banned all private vehicles from city streets during almost all daylight hours. That meant passenger coaches, delivery wagons, and other non-government vehicles could drive only early in the morning or at night.

At least two hundred fifty people were required to operate a dromon. Most of the crew manned the oars, while the rest served as soldiers in combat.

for hurling stones at enemies and pirates. Other ships had movable bridges that allowed soldiers to board enemy vessels.

The *dromon* was the greatest Roman warship. The Roman Empire used the dromon after the fourth century CE. This swift vessel had sails, banks of rowers, and tough armor made from leather and cloth. The armor was soaked with vinegar and other fluids. These liquids kept ships from catching on fire when hit by hot stones or flaming arrows.

CONCLUSION
After the Ancients

Ancient civilizations arose and flourished. Then they fell or other groups conquered them. But even after a civilization died out, its technology often remained. Through trade or conquest, other civilizations built on the knowledge of past peoples to further develop technology.

Many historians mark the collapse of the Roman Empire in 476 CE as the point at which Western Europe entered a new period called the Middle Ages. Roman roads began to deteriorate because no one maintained them. Even so, they remained the best roads in Europe for centuries. Not a single new highway was built in Europe for more than five hundred years after Rome fell.

Progress in mapmaking slowed during Europe's Middle Ages, but copies continued to be made of ancient maps. Few original ancient maps survived this period. We have only copies of most ancient maps. We don't know how accurately early scholars followed the originals. It's possible that each scholar added personal artistic touches.

Advances in transportation did not stop completely after the fall of the Roman Empire. For instance, Europeans learned more about ancient boat making and began to develop their own ships. In the late thirteenth century and early fourteenth century, Italian traveler Marco Polo sailed to central Asia and China. In 1298 he praised the Chinese bulkhead system for its stability. Polo noted that even if a ship "springs a leak by running against a rock, or on being hit by a hungry whale," bulkheads prevent it from sinking. Surprisingly, European boatbuilders didn't adopt bulkheads until the nineteenth century.

Rediscovery

In the fourteenth century, Europeans took a greater interest in the learning, literature, art, and technology of the ancient world. This led to a period of great creativity and invention called the Renaissance (1300s–1600). Renaissance means "rebirth."

Leonardo da Vinci (1452–1519) was a gifted Italian painter, sculptor, mathematician, and inventor. He produced some of the first known designs for flying machines. The machines were never built in Leonardo's lifetime. Modern scientists doubt whether they would fly, but the designs influenced future generations. One resembled a motorless helicopter and another a hang glider.

Leonardo may have been inspired by an earlier mind. According to second century CE Roman writer Aulus Gellius, the Greek mathematician Archytas developed a bird-shaped flying craft during the 300s BCE. The craft, called the *Pigeon*, reportedly traveled across short distances while suspended on a wire.

The Age of Discovery

The Renaissance coincided with an era known as the Age of Discovery. Throughout the fifteenth and sixteenth centuries, explorers from Europe traveled the sea in search of new trade routes and goods that were hard to find in Europe. For many European nations, the Age of Discovery marked the start of regular contact with Asia and Africa. And though the Vikings had visited North America over four hundred years earlier, the era also marked the start of regular European visits to North and South America.

In the fifteenth century, Middle Eastern traders learned about the compass from the Chinese. Compass technology soon spread to Europe. This tool helped make possible such sea voyages as Christopher Columbus's trips to the so called "New World" (as opposed to the "Old World" of Europe). Columbus, an Italian explorer working for Spain, arrived in the Americas in 1492. He had been sailing west across the Atlantic, looking for a new route to India. Columbus used maps based on the designs of Claudius Ptolemy, a second century geographer from Alexandria, which were not the most accurate by the time of Columbus and miscalculated the circumference of Earth. They also did not include the Americas, because few Europeans knew about their existence.

The Columbian Exchange

New technology is almost always beneficial. It helps people live healthier, happier, longer lives. However, almost all new technology has effects nobody could have foreseen. That is true for transportation technology as well.

After Christopher Columbus's trip to the Americas in 1492, advances in navigation and other transportation technology encouraged more trans-Atlantic voyages. That led to a massive exchange of goods, plants, animals, and ideas between the so-called Old and New Worlds. We call this the Columbian Exchange.

Unfortunately, this exchange also included the exchange of diseases. Sailors brought germs with them, such as measles and influenza. Indigenous Americans had no immunity to these diseases. Mind-boggling epidemics swept through the Indigenous population. Between 1492 and 1650, nearly ninety percent of Indigenous Americans had died. On some Caribbean islands, no Indigenous people survived.

One result was a drastic shortage of workers available for colonial farms and plantations. As demands for labor grew in colonial farms and plantations, Europeans began capturing and enslaving Africans to provide free labor in the Americas. This capture and enslavement of people, called the Atlantic slave trade, began in 1480. It only ended in the nineteenth century when Great Britain, the United States, and other countries around the world finally outlawed the trading of enslaved people.

The Industrial Revolution

In the mid-eighteenth century, Europe entered an era known as the Industrial Revolution. During this period, improvements in power-driven machines allowed people to produce goods more quickly and in larger amounts than they could by hand. Across Europe, large factories opened. Many people moved from farms to cities.

Many of the first steam engines were used to pump water out of mines.

Changes in the way people made goods demanded new ways to transport goods and the materials used to make them. Engineers developed new ways to pave roads, such as laying down thin layers of crushed rock. These new roads were smoother, and vehicles traveled across them faster.

Several ancient inventors had built simple steam engines. A Greek mathematician named Hero of Alexandria wrote about his engine in Egypt in the first century CE. But in 1769 Scottish engineer James Watt perfected the modern steam engine.

Watt's invention soon powered both vehicles and factory machinery. In 1804 British engineer Richard Trevithick built the first steam locomotive, an engine-powered vehicle designed for railways. Workers built and laid thousands of miles of railroad track through Britain and beyond. In 1807 US inventor Robert Fulton built a practical steam-powered boat. Fulton's boat was able to travel much faster than most boats without engines. Within a few decades, steamboats were making regular trips across the Atlantic Ocean.

Changes on Land and in the Air

For centuries after Leonardo da Vinci dreamed up his flying machines, people continued to think about flight. In 1783 French inventors created the first flying hot air balloons capable of carrying human passengers. In the nineteenth century, several inventors in the United States and Europe built gliders, crafts that could fly short distances on wind currents. Motor-powered flight craft emerged by the early twentieth century following innovations from American inventors Wilbur and Orville Wright and others. A couple of decades later, people were producing airplanes on a massive scale.

The motor-powered automobile arrived in the nineteenth century. As with flying machines, no single person is responsible for the automobile. In 1885 German inventor Karl Benz built the first wheeled vehicle to run solely on gasoline. In 1908 US inventor Henry Ford designed the Model T, the first automobile that most middle-class Americans could afford. Ford also devised assembly lines, a way for factories to quickly produce large numbers of automobiles. The work of Benz, Ford, and others depended on many ancient innovations, such as wheels joined by axles and made from multiple parts.

The automobile led to the creation of modern highway systems. From road signs to rest stops to the organizations needed to maintain them, modern highways have much in common with the roadways of ancient Rome and ancient India. We can still walk or drive on parts of ancient roads today, such as the Appian Way.

Looking Backward

Much of modern transportation technology may seem unconnected with ancient times, such as cars or airplanes. But the vehicles that move us today owe a huge debt to discoveries thousands of years ago. Without the invention of the wheel four thousand years ago, the world would come to a stop. Forget about motor vehicles, airplanes, and machines that use wheel-shaped gears. Horses remained the main form of personal transportation in the world until the early twentieth century. The modern wheelbarrow shares its basic design with the wooden ox of ancient China. Modern skis and snowshoes likewise take the same shapes as their ancient versions.

We still are fascinated with ancient transportation technology. That's why people try to re-create it and learn from it. In 1987 a group of historians and architects called the Trireme Trust built a full-size replica of an ancient Greek trireme warship. The group took the ship on several test voyages. By constructing its own trireme, the Trireme Trust learned more about how quickly Greek ships could move and how much power it took to move them.

TIMELINE

ca. 10,000 BCE	People begin to form permanent villages and domesticate animals.
ca. 4000 BCE	The earliest known civilization, Sumer, appears in Mesopotamia. People in the Middle East tame wild horses.
ca. 3000 BCE	The Phoenicians introduce sails on their gauloi.
ca. 2000 BCE	Riding on horseback becomes popular in the Middle East. Inventors in Mesopotamia develop the spoked wheel.
ca. 1400 BCE	Egyptian woodworkers make wheels with separate rims, spokes, and hubs.
1200s BCE	Egyptian engineers dig a canal that allows ships to pass from the Mediterranean Sea to the Red Sea.
ca. 500 BCE	Persian king Darius I orders the building of a waterway to the Red Sea.
486 BCE	Construction begins on China's Grand Canal.
312 BCE	Appius Claudius Caecus conceives a system of roads across the Roman Empire.
ca. 300 BCE	Indian horse riders begin using stirrups.
ca. 280 BCE	Greek ruler Ptolemy II orders the construction of the Pharos of Alexandria.
476 CE	The Western Roman Empire falls to invaders. Western Europe enters the Middle Ages.
1300s	Europe enters the Renaissance.
1400s	The Age of Discovery begins.
1500s	European explorers begin regular travel to the Americas.
1700s	The Age of Discovery ends, and the Industrial Revolution begins.
1769	Scottish inventor James Watt perfects the steam engine.
1804	British inventor Richard Trevithick builds the first steam locomotive.

1807	American engineer Robert Fulton builds the first commercially successful steam-powered boat.
1885	German engineer Karl Benz builds the first wheeled vehicle to run solely on gasoline.
1908	American industrialist Henry Ford designs the Model T.
1987	The Trireme Trust oversees the building of a full-size Greek trireme. They sail it to learn more about the practicality and speed of the ancient trireme.
2009	Archaeologists discover ancient stone tools on the island of Crete that raise questions about the earliest dates of extended boat travel.
2010	Archaeologists in Armenia discover the world's oldest known leather shoe.

GLOSSARY

archaeologist: a scientist who studies the remains of past human cultures

artifact: a human-made object, especially one characteristic of a certain group or historical period

axle: a rod in the center of a wheel

barge: a long boat with a flat bottom

bulkhead: a solid wall on the body of a boat made from wooden planks

canal: a channel that is dug across land to connect bodies of water

canoe: a narrow boat powered by paddling

cardinal points: the four principal compass points—north, south, east, and west

chariot: a small, wheeled vehicle pulled by one or more animals, usually horses

compass: a device with a magnetic needle that is used to determine direction

cuneiform: a writing system developed in the ancient Middle East, consisting of wedge-shaped characters

domesticate: to adapt an animal or a plant for human benefit

fiber-optic cable: a cable containing glass strands that carries light signals

hunter-gatherers: people who obtain their food by hunting, fishing, and gathering wild plants

irrigate: to supply (land, crops, etc.) with water by artificial means

junk: a boxy Chinese ship with a flat bottom, a high rear, and a low front

kelek: an Assyrian raft made from inflated sheepskins under a wooden frame

masula: an Indian boat or group of boats with planks and frames bound by rope

navigation: following a specific route with a map, compass, or computer

outrigger: a ship with a beam extending from its side to support a central mast

port: a place where boats and ships can dock

raft: a floating platform made from bound logs

rudder: a large underwater plate at the back of a boat or a ship, used for steering

sledge: a flat vehicle such as a sleigh, used to drag objects across the ground

stirrup: a loop that hangs from a horse's saddle into which a rider places their feet for balance and ease of mounting

travois: a vehicle consisting of two poles and sometimes an attached sled, dragged by a person or an animal across the ground

trireme: a Greek battleship, typically with three banks of rowers

yoke: a pole carried across the shoulder, used to transport items

SOURCE NOTES

29   "I ordered that . . . to my will." Andrew Robert Burn, *Persia and the Greeks: The Defence of the West*, c. 546–478 B.C. 2nd ed. (Stanford, CA: Stanford University Press, 1984), 115.

55   "[W]hat a size . . . a small army." Lucian of Samosata, *The Works of Lucian of Samosata, vol. 4*, trans. Henry Watson Fowler and Francis George Fowler (Oxford, UK: Clarendon Press, 1905), 35.

60   "Appia teritur regina longarum viarum." John August Hare, *Walks in Rome* (New York: Macmillan, 1903), 297.

64   "springs a leak by running against a rock, or on being hit by a hungry whale . . ." Thomas Ask, *Handbook of Marine Surveying* (Dobbs Ferry, NY: Sheridan House, 2007), 109.

SELECTED BIBLIOGRAPHY

Aust, Siegfried. *Ships! Come Aboard*. Minneapolis: Lerner Publications Company, 1993.

Barbieri-Low, Anthony. "Wheeled Vehicles in the Chinese Bronze Age (c. 2000–741 b.c.)." *Sino-Platonic Papers* 99 (February 2000).

Casson, Lionel. *Ships and Seamanship in the Ancient World*. Baltimore: Johns Hopkins University Press, 1995.

Cotterell, Arthur. *China's Civilization: A Survey of Its History, Arts and Technology*. New York: Praeger, 1975.

Gardiner, Robert, ed. *The Earliest Ships: The Evolution of Boats into Ships*. Annapolis, MD: Naval Institute Press, 1996.

Humble, Richard. *Ships: Sailors and the Sea*. New York: Franklin Watts, 1991.

James, Peter, and Nick Thorpe. *Ancient Inventions*. New York: Ballantine, 1994.

Johnstone, Paul. *The Seacraft of Prehistory*. Cambridge, MA: Harvard University Press, 1980.

Kerrod, Robin. *Transportation: From the Bicycle to Spacecraft*. New York: Macmillan, 1991.

"Legacy of the Horse." International Museum of the Horse. December 8, 1998. http://imh.org/legacy-of-the-horse (August 19, 2010).

Perry, Marvin. *A History of the Ancient World*. Boston: Houghton Mifflin, 1985.

Saggs, H. W. F. *Civilization Before Greece and Rome*. New Haven, CT: Yale University Press, 1989.

Starr, Chester G., Jr., ed. *A History of the Ancient World*. New York: Oxford University Press, 1991.

White, K. D. *Greek and Roman Technology*. Ithaca, NY: Cornell University Press, 1984.

Wilkinson, Philip, ed. *Early Humans*. New York: Knopf, 1989.

FURTHER READING

Books

Jackson, Tom. *Wonders of the World*. New York: DK Publishing, 2022.
Explore over fifty historical wonders in this illustrated guide to
the natural and human-made wonders of the world, including the
Great Pyramids of Giza and the Great Lighthouse of Alexandria.

Miller, Tessa. *Wings & Beaks: Technology Inspired by Animals*.
Minneapolis: Full Tilt Press, 2019.
From dragonfly drones to sonar, humans have been inspired
to make new technologies mimicking flying creatures. This
book shows how nature has inspired human machinery
throughout history.

West, David. *Warships*. New York: Crabtree Publishing Company, 2020.
Warships have been used throughout history to transport soldiers
and control the seas. This book explores the history of warships
from Greek triremes to modern destroyers.

Woods, Mary B and Michael. *Construction through the Ages*.
Minneapolis: Twenty-First Century Books, 2025.
Machines throughout history have been used to construct
everything from houses to monuments. Learn the history of
ancient construction techniques and the technology behind them.

Wyse, Elizabeth. *A History of the Classical World*. London:
Arcturus, 2021.
Greece and Rome both controlled vast empires in the ancient
world. This illustrated book explores the history of the rise of
both empires, along with information about their architecture, art,
and politics.

Websites

National Geographic: 10 Ancient Highways Around the World
  https://www.nationalgeographic.com/travel/article/ancient
  -highways
  This article from National Geographic magazine lists ten famous
  transportation routes from before the invention of the automobile.

PBS LearningMedia: The Columbian Exchange
  https://www.pbslearningmedia.org/resource/midlit11.soc.splcol/
  the-columbian-exchange/
  Explore how ocean travel facilitated the Columbian Exchange in
  this interactive lesson from PBS.

Phoenician Ships, Boats and Sea Trade
  http://www.phoenician.org/ancient_ships.htm
  Learn more about the influential boat-making techniques of the
  ancient Phoenicians.

UNESCO: About the Silk Roads
  https://en.unesco.org/silkroad/about-silk-roads
  This article explores the many trade networks that came together
  to form the Silk Road and the goods, languages, ideas, and
  cultures that traveled along them.

INDEX

Age of Discovery. *See Renaissance*
airplanes, 5 *See flying machines*
Americas
  canoes, 10–11, 43, 48–50
  Inca, 47
  Maya, 49–50
  Mesoamerica, 49
  North America, 44–46, 48, 65
  Olmec, 50–51
Appian Way, 60, 69
Ashoka, emperor of India, 39
automobiles, 68–69

boats
  Americas, 48–49
  Chinese, 34–35
  early, 9–11
  Egyptian, 25–26, 29
  Greek, 55
  Indian, 43
  Middle Eastern, 17–19
  Roman, 61
  steam-powered, 68
bridges, 5, 47, 60, 62

canals, 29–33, 50
canoes, 10–11, 43, 48–50
China
  canals, 32–33
  compass, 65
  junks, 33–36
  Silk Road, 36–37, 42
  wheelbarrow, 35–36, 69
compass, 65

domesticated animals (beasts of burden), 11–12, 21, 23, 39, 46, 49

Egypt
  boats, 25–26, 29
  Khufu, 27
  maps, 27
  paved roads, 30–31
  seafaring vessels, 26
  sledges, 30–31
  Suez Canal, 29–30
elephants, 11, 39–41

flying machines, 64, 68–69
footwear, 8, 9 *See also shoes*
freighters, 19, 56

gauloi (round sailboat), 19
Great Pyramid, 27
Greece
  freighters, 56
  navigation and mapmaking, 52, 57
  Pharos of Alexandria, 53–54
  Ptolemy, 53, 65
  triremes, 55, 69

horses, 11–12, 20–23, 36–37, 41–42, 46, 61, 69

Inca, 47
India
  Ashoka, 39
  boats, 43
  elephants, 39–41
  horses, 41–42
Industrial Revolution, 66–69

junks, 33–36

keleks (inflatable boats), 17–18
Khufu (pharaoh), 27

land bridge, 44

mapmaking, 52, 57, 63
maps, 5, 27, 57, 60–61, 63, 65
Maya, 49–50
Mediterranean Sea, 12, 16, 26, 29–30, 37, 52–53, 61
Mesopotamia, 16, 19, 22–23, 57, 59
Middle Ages, 63
Middle East
  Assyrians, 16–18
  Babylonians, 16, 57
  boats, 17–19
  horses, 20–21, 23
  Mesopotamia, 16, 22–23, 57
  Phoenicians, 16, 19
  sails, 19–20
  Sumerians, 16

navigation, 26, 66 *See also maps*
Nile River, 24–26, 29–31, 56
North America, 44–46, 48, 65

Olmec, 50–51

Paleo-Indians, 45
Peutinger Table, 61
Pharos of Alexandria, 53–54
Phoenicians, 16, 19
ports, 5, 16, 24, 29, 50
Ptolemy, 53, 65
pyramids, 27, 30–31 *See also Great Pyramid*

Red Sea, 29–30
Renaissance, 64–65
roads, 5–6, 12–13, 30–31, 37, 47, 58–61, 63, 67, 69
  Roman, 58–61, 63
  See also Silk Road

Rome
  Appius Claudis Caecus, 59
  Appius Claudius Caecus, 59
  roads, 58–61, 63
  traffic laws, 61
  warships, 61–62

sails, 5, 11, 19–20, 25–26, 29, 35, 56, 62
shoes, 8–9, 48, 69
Silk Road, 36–37, 42
skis, 14, 48, 69
sledges, 12, 14–15, 30–31, 51
snowshoes, 48, 69
steam engine, 67
stirrups, 42
Suez Canal, 29–30

technology
  ancient roots, 4
  defined, 4
  transportation, 5–6, 8, 11, 16, 21–22, 32, 35, 40–41, 45, 49, 52, 64–66, 69
traffic laws, 61
travois, 12, 15, 45–46

Via Appia, 60 *See Appian Way*

warships, 19–20, 29, 61–62
wheelbarrow, 35–36, 69
wheels and axles, 49

yokes, 12, 45

ABOUT THE AUTHORS

Michael Woods is a science and medical journalist in Washington, DC. He has won many national writing awards. Mary B. Woods is a school librarian. Their past books include the fifteen–volume *Disasters Up Close* series and many titles in the *Seven Wonders* series. The Woodses have four children. When not writing, reading, or enjoying their seven grandchildren, the Woodses travel to gather material for future books.

PHOTO ACKNOWLEDGMENTS

DEA/M. SEEMULLER/Getty Images, p. 5; DEA/G. DAGLI ORTI/Getty Images, p. 8; Transcendental Graphics/Getty Images, p. 10; Steve Taylor ARPS/Alamy, p. 13; omersukrugoksu/Getty Images, p. 17; Science & Society Picture Library/Getty Images, p. 18; 67 Izzet Keribar/Getty Images, p. 20; skaman306/Getty Images, p. 25; Werner Forman/Getty Images, p. 26; AMIR MAKAR/Getty Images, p. 28; Ancient Art and Architecture/Alamy, p. 31; xijian/Getty Images, p. 33; RichLegg/Getty Images, p. 34; RNMitra/Getty Images, p. 37; Tibor Bognar/Getty Images, p. 39; Gianni Dagli Orti/Shutterstock, p. 40; ephotocorp/Alamy, p. 42; Planet One Images/Getty Images, p. 43; Kypros/Getty Images, p. 45; H. Armstrong Roberts/ClassicStock/Getty Images, p. 46; Joerg Steber/Getty Images, p. 47; marekuliasz/Getty Images, p. 48; Michael Godek/Getty Images, p. 51; Print Collector/Getty Images, p. 53; NurPhoto/Getty Images, p. 54; Heritage Images/Getty Images, p. 57; Print Collector/Getty Images, p. 59; Bildagentur-online/Getty Images, p. 62

Cover image: Heritage Images/Getty Images